Operating in the

God-kind

of

Faith

Sebastian D. Weaver

Operating in the

God-kind

Of

Faith

Sebastian D. Weaver

Operating in the God-kind of Faith
ISBN-13: 978-0615910178
ISBN-10: 0615910173

Printed by CreateSpace, an Amazon.com Company

Dedication

I dedicate this book to my wife, Jill, who allowed me the time necessary to focus on this project and has participated in helping bring it to completion. From the initial conception, to the long hours of structuring, writing and editing, she has been there as a counselor, confidant and cheerleader.

Throughout the many years of our marriage, I could always count on her to be the "better part" of me. She has always encouraged me to follow the "leadings" of the Lord, even when other people thought I was losing it. Therefore, I am grateful and thankful for the gift she is to me and love her so much.

Table of Contents

Introduction

The Importance of Faith

"But without faith it is impossible to please him: for he that cometh to God must believe that he is, and that he is a rewarder of them that diligently seek him." —Hebrews 11:6

Faith for a Christian is a firm persuasion, conviction, or trust in another. This definition when added to the above scripture is the very foundation from which I preach and teach others to practice faith and trust in the Lord. Faith and trust can be used interchangeably. I believe that our faith or trust in God and Jesus should not stop with praying the Sinner's Prayer. Our faith in God is why we are called Believers.

The Christian Believer is: *"One who gives credit to the truth of the Scriptures, as a revelation from God. A Christian—in a more restricted sense—is one who receives Christ as his Savior and accepts the way of salvation revealed in the gospel"* (*Webster's Dictionary—1828*). In other words, this believing is a person's expression of their faith in God and His Word, to receive Christ into his or her heart as their personal Savior; with the desire to live a life committed to the truth of God's Holy Word.

1

Faith, and the need for it, should be Christianity 101 for every Believer. Anyone who dares to say they are a devoted follower of Christ needs to know or understand that God requires us to walk by and live a life of faith. To live for and serve God, there must be a desire to please him and it takes faith to accomplish that. Now someone may say, 'I don't have any faith'...I have an answer for them. YES you do!!

We all have faith—the Bible says we do. Romans 12:3 tell us that God has *"dealt to every man the measure of faith."* We exercise our ability to have faith every day in many ways and we even talk about having faith in this or that. In the natural, we will sit in a chair confident that it will hold us. We will express faith in the word of a trusted friend or family member, without any reason to trust them at all. Furthermore, we will accept a job and begin to work because someone has promised to pay us. All of these are expressions of faith or trust.

In our natural everyday lives, we express faith in all sorts of things. So, spiritually speaking, it should not be hard to accept that we must have and express faith when it comes to the things of God. Also, it is important to note that if we can have faith in people and non-living objects, like chairs, surely we should have faith in the God who created us.

In the Bible, we have sixty-six books which describe God's love for us. It also shows His faithfulness and His willingness to show Himself strong on our behalf. Time after time, in the Bible, we see God moving on behalf of the people who believe in Him. Hence it is to our advantage, and I dare say our responsibility, to exercise our faith in God fully every day without reservation. We do this because He loves us, has a plan for us and has given us the very best of Himself. We can do this by turning our full attention to the reading of God's Word, in faith, with the intent to hear, learn, and obey.

"And Jesus replied to him, it is written, Man shall not live and be sustained by (on) bread alone but by every word and expression of God." —Luke 4:4 (Amplified)

Our entire lives are tied to our faith in and faithfulness to the Spirit-breathed Word of the Living God! Therefore, it is imperative to understand that God has provided for us everything "*that pertain unto life and godliness, through...exceeding great and precious promises*;" (2 Peter 1:3-4). We must trust and have confidence in Him and His willingness to give us His best at all times and in every circumstance. Do not make the mistake of stopping at the door of the goodness of God, and never fully enjoying all He has given us through faith in Him—we must have faith in God!

Chapter 1

Why Study Faith?

1-2"The fundamental fact of existence is that this trust in God, this faith, is the firm foundation under everything that makes life worth living. It's our handle on what we can't see. The act of faith is what distinguished our ancestors, set them above the crowd."—Hebrews 11:1-2 (The Message)

I lived as a Christian and even served in the ministry for many years without understanding probably the most basic concept in the Bible—Faith! Faith as a living, working truth was not something on which I had a firm grasp. To me it is amazing how many Christians are living pretty much the same way. Many are good at confessing or declaring their faith in God but miss out on the fact that God intends for them to live by that same faith.

To live by faith is to allow your confidence in God, His love, and His power, to guide and fulfill your life.

I make this statement because of the frustration that is evident among many in the Body of Christ—a sense of powerlessness over the circumstances of life. This frustration comes from, I believe, a lack of knowledge or understanding of not only what the Bible is saying to the Believer but what it means as well.

Faith in God is an empowerment to reach beyond ourselves (our natural lives), and tap into the power and provision of an almighty God.

When Jesus told His disciples to *"Have faith in God,"* (Mark 11:22), He was saying for them to make a transformation in the way they had been thinking about and seeing life.

"Do not conform yourselves to the standards of this world, but let God transform you inwardly by a complete change of your mind. Then you will be able to know the will of God—what is good and is pleasing to him and is perfect." — Romans 12:2 (Good News Translation)

Only God can transform us. Many of us have spent our lives trying to change, break habits, and be a better person and so on. But it is only when we allow our minds to be renewed to the ways of God that we will really see a difference—I believe this is what Jesus was teaching the disciples.

Surely, they were accustomed to things operating in a natural, human way of living and being. They had learned "life's lessons" in their upbringing…that was limited at best. Our lives are limited due to being dependent upon the things and understanding of this natural earth and mankind.

Limits are taught to us from infancy. We are told how much we can do or have and how far we can go. We are told what we can or cannot afford. We are even told what we should be afraid of. But Jesus wanted them and us to know that there are no limits in God—for His power is supernatural. He wants us to know nothing is impossible when we place unwavering faith in God!

Life Lesson

Recently, I had a conversation with one of my sons. He lovingly reminded me of some limitations that were imbedded in his head because of some of the things I taught him. I apologized but I also told him: as an adult he was now responsible to use God's Word to evaluate the things he learned as a child and make the appropriate adjustment. In other words, I wanted him to know: although, we may have unknowingly planted seeds in him that created fear or doubt; it was now his responsibility to turn to God, choose the path of obedience and faith, and not to make excuses.

No More Excuses

Now, I understand our parents meant well; you and I mean well also when we do the same to our children. But it is important to note that things taught in error, even with the best of intentions, is still incorrect. Just because we have learned something from our beloved parents, life teachers or spiritual leaders, does not mean it was right and definitely should be reevaluated for accuracy before we pass it on. Faith in God, in every aspect of our lives, is the lesson we should both learn and teach. Remember: *"...the just shall live by his faith."* (Habakkuk 2:4)

To live by faith is to live by the power of the Word of God—who cannot fail.

The Word of God contains His plan for our lives; *"For I know the thoughts that I think toward you, says the Lord, thoughts of peace and not of evil, to give you a future and a hope."* (Jeremiah 29:11 - NKJV). It is tapping into and following that plan is what will turn our lives from average to extraordinary! It will answer questions that have been shrouded in a cloud of mystery for far too long. The mystery is there because throughout the ages, men have created their own rationalization for those things they don't understand instead of turning to the Word of God—which has the answers.

To choose to live by faith is to take away the excuses and make the decision to trust God above all else!

When you look at it, trusting God for our daily lives is more important than breathing. I know that sounds a bit over-the-top but it is just that significant.

Bread is more than Food

"Jesus answered by quoting Deuteronomy: It takes more than bread to stay alive. It takes a steady stream of words from God's mouth."— Matthew 4:4 (The Message)

It has been said, "We are what we eat". This suggests: our lives are a direct indication of our diet. Now, the natural and physical implication of that statement is unmistakable but I am dealing more with the spiritual implications of what we eat. The things we focus upon, dwell upon and talk about are the things that are directly related to our condition spiritually and even the tangible things of our lives as well. Consider this:

"The light of the body is the eye: if therefore thine eye be single, thy whole body shall be full of light. But if thine eye be evil, thy whole body shall be full of darkness. If therefore the light that is in thee be darkness, how great is that darkness!"—Matthew 6:22-23

It is very important we realize what we focus upon—good or bad—will have a direct impact upon the quality of our lives. When we give our attention to things that are full of doubt, worry, and fear—our lives will mirror that and we will be full of those types of things.

For instance, if we focus on some news report of an increase in crime in our area, we will begin to become conditioned to the possibility of being a victim of some sort of crime and begin to worry about "when" it will happen to us. This is what I call becoming spiritually conditioned to a thing—whether good or bad. You can use the same scenario and duplicate it in all aspects of our lives—our finances, health, family, and so on.

Take our health for instance. When we look at television, especially at certain times of day, all we see are commercials convincing us of how sick we are and what medications will help us get well. Before long, when we would feel that ache, pain, or any other 'symptom' that we have been bombarded with, we will begin to believe we may have that condition. My friend that should never happen but it does all too often.

God has given us guidelines from which to live and that is by "the word of God." It is by spending time in and focusing on His word that we will be transformed in the *"image of His Son."* (Romans 8: 29). You see, in Matthew chapter 4, when Satan came to tempt Jesus; he tried to get Him to be so concerned over His own natural needs (food for hunger), that he told Him to make stones into bread to provide for His own needs—but Jesus had an answer for that devil. Jesus' answer was pure and simple: "...it is written..." and that should be our answer to every adverse circumstance in life!

The only way we can take a stand and state emphatically: "it is written" is to spend time in the Word of God long enough to allow it to nourish us like natural bread would curb hunger. Natural food is a sustainer of our natural selves...so is the Word of God for our spiritual selves. We need God's Word to live and to overcome this world and its system of fear, lack, prejudices, hate, sickness, etc. There is no natural answer for the ills of this life— we need faith in God's Word.

Regardless of where we turn or what we do, we need God and His Word every day and every hour without fail to live successful and victorious lives. Now, unfortunately we have been trained and conditioned to go about our lives without fully trusting in God. But it is only the mercy of God, according to scripture, that is why we are not consumed. The Lord looks after us even if we are not looking to Him. But that is not His best for us. So we need God and we must trust in him if we are going to have any real quality of life.

"Cursed are those who put their trust in mere humans, who rely on human strength and turn their hearts away from the Lord."—Jeremiah 17:5 (New Living Translation)

It is significant to note here that many people do achieve things in their own lives because they have worked hard and have trusted in themselves. But it is interesting also to note that many people who have worked hard and who do trust in themselves are not happy. Many of them have failing marriages, a failing family, failing health and ultimately they lose everything important because they did it themselves. We as believers must put our trust in God and not in ourselves. We must put our trust in God and not in men. Psalms 118.8 says "*it is better to trust in the Lord than to put confidence in man...*"

The most important thing we can do as Christians is to bury our entire selves in our faith in The Lord. I will dare to say, our entire life depends upon it. God has stated in His Word that the "just shall live by faith." How can we continue living lives which are dependent upon the systems of this world (political/government, health /medical resources, economic/stock markets, etc.), and expect those systems which are ungodly systems, to do for us what God and He alone can do for us?

"Study to shew thyself approved unto God, a workman that needeth not to be ashamed, rightly dividing the word of truth." (2 Timothy 2:15)

For the Believer, it is imperative to study the subject of faith. What's more, it is imperative that we make it our life's mission to understand the importance of faith in our lives. This is the starting point to walking a life that is pleasing to God. Please remember this:

"But without faith it is impossible to please him: for he that cometh to God must believe that he is, and that he is a rewarder of them that diligently seek him."—Hebrews 11:6

It is impossible to please Him if we don't know Him; and we cannot possibly know Him or His character without faith in Him.

Chapter 2

Faith in God's Love

"For God so loved the world that he gave his only begotten Son, that whosoever believeth in him should not perish, but have everlasting life."—John 3:16

Most of us have heard this verse throughout our lives. Some have heard it in church, at home or in many other places, including seeing it on signs at sporting events. But have you ever taken notice of the power within this verse of scripture? It speaks of God, His Son (Jesus), the world (or we within it), believers in Him, and our quality—not length—of life.

When this verse is often heard, it gives the impression of God wanting everyone to go to heaven. But why is that the case? Is it because this verse, or some variation of it, has been preached or taught that way? Many Christians have the opinion: the purpose of the sacrifice of Jesus on the Cross was just so we can go to heaven as an eternal destination. However, when this verse is read, it talks about the love of God for everyone; and that love has a purpose!

God's Love Has a Purpose

I believe the Bible as a whole, teaches us about God's love for us, and His willingness to see us live a life of victory and not defeat. The victory that God gives includes both our natural and spiritual lives. In the spiritual, it is clear that God wanted us to come to Him and live with and for Him eternally— where He will be our God and we will be His people (Genesis 17:8).

This is important because God never intended to be separated from us. In the Garden however, sin drove man from the presence of God and limited His power in our lives. Jesus was sent to "bridge" the gap—so to speak—to do for us what we could not do for ourselves. Jesus, through the shedding of His blood, redeemed (or bought), us back to God (Galatians 3:13). The scriptures also teach: God loved us so much that, while we were still lost in sin and would have stayed that way, Christ gave his life for us (Romans 5:8).

This sacrifice was given as a gift to us and assists us in the life we live daily by faith in that sacrifice. Our faith or belief in Jesus' death as payment for our sin and His resurrection from the dead; gives us power to be saved or delivered by faith. Therefore, Salvation frees us from all of the ills brought upon this earth and humanity by the stain of sin. That is a strong statement, I know, but which would you rather believe…that all things are possible through faith in God (Matthew 19:26 & Luke 1:37), or some things are left to chance? I don't believe God left anything to chance—neither should we.

Consider how the love of God was essential for redemption after the fall of mankind. There was no way for man to have any chance at all, were it not for God Himself extending forgiveness and redemption through the shed blood of Jesus. His blood would cleanse everyone who would accept Him into their hearts by faith.

The Bible teaches us that all things are held up *"by the word of His power"* (Hebrews 1:3). It also teaches that because we are "crucified with Christ", He lives within us and this life we are living here on earth is lived by our faith in Jesus' obedient sacrifice and through the love of God (Galatians 2:20)! What does this all mean? Simply, God loved us so much that He gave His all to cure us from the dreadful disease of sin!

If He would provide for us the cure for sin, then why wouldn't He also with it provide the cure for everything else that ails us in this life, (sickness, poverty, lack, relationship trouble, etc.,)—The love of God covers all!

Read Romans 8:32 in the following translations:

- "Since he did not spare even his own Son but gave him up for us all, won't he also give us everything else?" (New Living Translation)

- "He who did not withhold or spare [even] His own Son but gave Him up for us all, will He not also with Him freely and graciously give us all [other] things?" (Amplified)

- "If God didn't hesitate to put everything on the line for us, embracing our condition and exposing himself to the worst by sending his own Son, is there anything else he wouldn't gladly and freely do for us?" (The Message)

- "He that spared not his own Son, but delivered him up for us all, how shall he not with him also freely give us all things?" (King James Version)

Chapter 3

Faith in God's Plan

"For I know the thoughts and plans that I have for you, says the Lord, thoughts and plans for welfare and peace and not for evil, to give you hope in your final outcome."—Jeremiah 29:11 (Amplified)

It is amazing how many Christians are good at acknowledging their faith in God, but miss out on the fact that God intends for them to live by that same faith (Romans 1:17). To live by faith is to allow your confidence in God, His love, and His power, to guide and fulfill your life. To live by faith is to live by the power of the Word of God...who cannot fail!

The Word of God contains His plan for our lives. To tap into that plan is what will turn our lives from average to extraordinary! It will answer questions that have been shrouded in a cloud of mystery for far too long. The mystery is there because throughout the ages, men have created their own explanation for those things they don't understand instead of turning to the Word of God...which has the answers. For instance, if a person were to get a 'bad report' from the doctor; they could turn to the Word of God and see that God says, I am the God that heals you (Exodus

15:26). Then choose to believe the Word and place it in higher priority than the report—this is what it means to live by faith.

There are two elements we have the choice to live by; one is facts and the other is truth. The doctor's report is based upon facts, but the Word is always truth and truth is higher than the facts—always! Jesus said, while praying in John 17:17, *"sanctify them through thy truth, thy word is truth"*. When faced with facts, grab the truth; find out what the Word says about the situation you are facing and stand on that instead of the facts!

Lest I be misunderstood, I did not say to ignore the facts but rather—believe the truth. In other words, believe in what God says more than whatever facts are screaming at you. Hold on to the Truth until the facts change. Regardless of what you are facing—the Truth will change the facts! This is putting your faith in action.

What does it mean to have faith in God?

22 "And Jesus answering saith unto them, Have faith in God. 23 For verily I say unto you, That whosoever shall say unto this mountain, Be thou removed, and be thou cast into the sea; and shall not doubt in his heart, but shall believe that those things which he saith shall come to pass; he shall have whatsoever he saith. 24 Therefore I say unto you, What things soever ye desire, when

18

ye pray, believe that ye receive them, and ye shall have them." Mark 11:21-24

To have faith in God is to exercise the faith given to us by God. For the scriptures declare that God has *"dealt to every man the measure of faith"* (Romans 12:3). Having faith in God is to have complete trust in God, His Word, His Will and His plan for our lives as being right and the right thing for us.

Furthermore, our faith in God can be determined by learning the kind of faith God expects. Now someone may be asking, "How can I know the faith God expects?" Well, the Bible—our guide for living the Christian life—is the Word of God and is full of examples of individuals who pleased God through their faith. This kind of faith is just as necessary today as it was then. Although times and technology have changed, God has not and His example is firm.

"Jesus Christ the same yesterday, and to day, and forever"—Hebrews 13:8

The Word of God, in the first chapter of Genesis, shows us that God spoke the world into existence and everything He spoke is still in operation today. It is the Creation narrative that shows us how God operated when He created the world and everything within it—this was all done by command through the spoken Word of God. He also has given us the authority to operate as He and we can command our world, through trusting in and speaking the Word in faith. Therefore, it is our responsibility to operate and live by the faith of God for: "...*The just shall live by faith*" (Romans 1:17).

To properly follow God by faith, we must use the power of the Word of God—coming out of our mouths—to make a difference in our lives as told in Proverbs 18:21, "*Death and life are in the power of the tongue.*" This difference can be made when we place our faith in the Word of God and recognize we have a say in the direction of our lives.

"(As it is written, I have made thee a father of many nations,) before him whom he believed, even God, who quickeneth the dead, and calleth those things which be not as though they were."—Romans 4:17

We do not have to accept things the way they are in our lives—we have the power to change our circumstances. Conditions are subject to God; therefore, they are subject to us. If we use the power given to us through the power of speech, we can take a hard situation and see life's situations turn around. How? By using the directive Jesus gave to the Apostles—"*Have faith in God*" (Mark 11:22).

In Romans 4 we are told of Abraham's faith in God and how he chose to believe what God says rather than believe what his body (circumstances) was telling him. Abraham's body was old (about 75 years old), when he met God. The Lord told him he would be the father of nations when he had yet to father one child. However, it was Abraham's faith in God's Word that propelled him into the future God promised. This tells us the importance of faith in our lives. Faith is absolutely necessary in the life of the Believer.

Faith in the Life of the Believer

"...Nevertheless when the Son of man cometh, shall he find faith on the earth?"—Luke 18:8

Faith is lacking in the daily lives of many Believers. This is because the subject of faith is largely misunderstood among Christians. Faith, like many other subjects (i.e. love), is used by many in various ways but often without understanding its true significance. Faith is the key to a victorious Christian life—this cannot be understated.

Four times the bible states that the "just shall live by faith." (Habakkuk 2:4; Romans 1:17; Galatians 3:11; Hebrews 10:38). The word just can be rendered righteous—thereby giving the interpretation that the righteous shall live by faith. Now please do not overlook the word live in these verses, because that little word live has great significance—especially in the believer's life of faith. To live is: to "be alive" and "to have life" but it compasses many other things as well. The dictionary defines to live as:

21

1. To spend, as one's life; to pass; to maintain; to continue in, constantly or habitually; as, to live an idle or a useful life.

2. To act habitually in conformity with; to practice. (*Webster's Revised Dictionary, 1828*)

When connected with the subject of faith, this brings to live to life...so to speak. Just imagine if we spent our life maintaining or continuing constantly and habitually in faith—thereby producing a useful life. Wow! How different would our lives be if we actually lived a life continuing constantly in faith rather than just talked about having it?

We serve a risen Savior who rose with all power in His hands; and then gave us the same power! Do not make the mistake of judging the power of God by the results or lack of results we have experienced in our lives. Faith is meant to produce in the life of a believer! A seed planted in the ground is planted to do one thing...produce! Faith in our lives has a job to do as well; and that is to produce the power of God in our lives.

The truth of the matter is: faith in the Word should be held to and practiced in order for us to experience its power and productivity. Jesus ridiculed the Sadducees by telling them *"...You're mistaken because you don't know the Scriptures or God's power"* (Matthew 22:29). Many Christians today are mistaken on the subject of faith because they don't know the Scriptures or God's power. God is able to take the simplest truths and promises in the Bible and make them a very real part of our lives—when we trust Him to do so.

Living by faith is learning what the Bible says about a thing, trusting that word as truth, believing and confessing (speaking) that it is yours now—not sometime in the future—and standing on that word until you experience it in reality! Faith, the Bible says, *"cometh by hearing"* the Word of God (Romans 10:17).

That hearing is not only with your natural ears but also with your heart. Living by and abiding in faith is not some snap of the finger exercise that you can get overnight. To have faith active in your life is an act of faith itself. First, you have to trust the Word of God that living and working faith is required for every Believer. Not only do the righteous have to live by faith, but it is impossible to please God without it (Hebrews 11:6).

The question asked by Jesus about finding "faith on the earth" in Luke 18:8 is not easily answered. The reason for this is due to a loss of the meaning and significance of Bible faith. The Bible says that God has given to *"every man the measure of faith."* (Romans 12:3). Faith is the tool that God has given us from which to use and operate. It is not the will of God for Believers to stand powerless and under the control of an enemy who would absolutely destroy us if allowed.

I know it is popular to hold to the belief that God is 'keeping us' and 'is in control'. But he also gave us the directive to *"occupy until I come"* (Luke 19:13). To occupy is to stay busy or employed. Realistically, it could be seen as giving your faith a job.

In other words, we are to take the faith He has given us and put it to use the same way a farmer would use seed. Farmers use seed to plant for an expected harvest. If a farmer wanted a corn crop, he would buy corn seed to plant. If he wanted beans to grow, he would buy bean seed and so on. After purchasing the seed, he would prepare the soil and plant the seed. He would not take the seed he has just purchased and put the bags in the barn and wait for it to produce!

Likewise, neither should we hold on to the seed of the Word that has been given us and hope it will produce in our lives. We must take that seed in faith and plant in the soil of our hearts daily, believing that it will produce the crop we believe for.

26 "And he said, So is the kingdom of God, as if a man should cast seed into the ground; 27 And should sleep, and rise night and day, and the seed should spring and grow up, he knoweth not how. 28 For the earth bringeth forth fruit of

herself; first the blade, then the ear, after that the full corn in the ear. 29 But when the fruit is brought forth, immediately he putteth in the sickle, because the harvest is come."—Mark 4:26-29

Again, using the example of the farmer, he works by faith also. The farmer has faith in the seed that is in the bag and in the soil he plants the seed in. He believes that when the seed is planted in 'good ground' and nourished properly, (sun, rain, fertilizer, etc.,), it will produce the crop it represents. Likewise, the Believer has the responsibility to take the seed of the Word of God, plant it in our hearts and nourish it properly with (prayer, praise, obedience, confession, love, etc.).

Comparatively, the heart of man is like the soil of the ground. Whenever seed is planted in the ground, the soil will begin its job to break down the shell of the seed so that the true seed can take root in the soil and grow. The heart or spirit of man is no different. When the seed of the Word of God is planted in our spirit, it then does what is necessary to cause that Word to grow and produce in us.

The farmer cannot make the seed he plants grow, but he does have the responsibility to plant it. Likewise, neither can we make the Word grow within us but we do have the responsibility to plant it in our hearts. Consequently, we should not just place our Bibles on the table and hope; because we have a Bible or go to church, we will learn what it says or that it would produce God's promises in our lives.

The Bible tells us that the *"just shall live by faith"* (Hebrews 10:38), and without it we cannot even *"please God"* (Hebrews 11:6). Think about trying to live a life pleasing to the Lord but missing it because we are neglecting the all-important aspect of dynamic faith. The life of faith is not just some group you belong to but it is a way of living. When we live by faith, we are not moved by the things that move everyone else. We are moved only by what we believe! And our believing has to be based on the Word. Why? Because believing in the Word produces God's power and provision in our lives.

Believers should live a life of faith! Believers who live by faith show everyone else how good God is—not just talk about it and sing songs about it! This is what makes us different from the rest of the world. The Word says, *"Greater is He that is in you, than he that is in the world."* (1 John 4:4). In other words, we have the greater one on the inside of us and producing His life in us!

The things that have everyone else 'shaking in their boots' should not to affect us one bit. Regardless of what may be going on around us, we can walk in protection by 'hiding' ourselves in God's 'shadow'; because the scripture tells us that *"A thousand shall fall at thy side, and ten thousand at thy right hand*" (Psalms 91:7); we can always triumph because we know in Whom we believe!

Chapter 4

Have Faith Not Fear

"For God hath not given us the spirit of fear; but of power, and of love, and of a sound mind."—2 Timothy 1:7 (KJV)

Fear is an enemy to faith. This is important to note because fear will strangle any effort to exercise faith in God and His Word. Fear is a luxury we absolutely cannot afford! Do not give in to fear; it is designed to torment us and to render us powerless in this world. We cannot play with fear, and 'a little fear' is not good for us under any circumstance. God is a god of faith and He expects His children to have faith and to walk in faith. In fact, because we are made in His image and His likeness, we should strive to live in and through faith, as we were made to do, in all aspects of our lives.

From the beginning, God expected man to take His Word and use its power to create our world. We read in Genesis 1:28 that God told man to *"be fruitful and multiply"* and empowered them to do so. Likewise, we still the same responsibility and it is following this mandate, through faith, that allows us to exercise the authority given to us by God. But when we allow everything that is 'anti-god' to rule over us, we subject ourselves to the very spirit of fear instead of faith.

Just as God has given us faith to use as His agents here on earth, Satan uses fear to paralyze the people of this earth into inactivity. It is fear that empowers the works of the enemy in our lives. Fear is something we can live without. As Christians, we should not want to possess anything God did not give us—naturally or spiritually. Understanding this bears great importance upon our experiencing the victory that comes with our Salvation. Jesus' sacrifice on the cross broke the curse of sin and death over our lives but we must access this through faith.

Satan uses the element of fear to keep us from receiving and walking in this life of victory. Fear is always at odds with faith. Faith in God and His Word brings us victory over all the ills of life (sickness, disease, poverty, despair, etc.). Fear keeps us connected to them and even draws more of the same to us! Remember this; fear is never good for us. Job found this out as noted below:

"The worst of my fears has come true, what I've dreaded most has happened. My repose is shattered, my peace destroyed. No rest for me, ever—death has invaded life."—Job 3:25-26 (Message)

Job experienced the power of fear in his life. The things he experienced was not as much God giving him over to the will of Satan for testing as it was Job's own fear opening the door and giving

Satan access! This is important to note because there are many Christians who see the challenges that Job faced as a godly thing and thereby accept their own challenges in the same way. Yes, we absolutely can learn something in any situation or circumstance. But please understand this, because it is in your life does not mean God placed it there or you in it. I understand we are sometimes taught these things but that does not make it right.

When we embrace fear, we welcome the very things we fear. Remember, there is nothing godly about fear. Fear is a killer, get rid of it! Do not allow fear to rest in you for one moment. It does not matter what the fear is: bills not getting paid, receiving a bad report from the doctor, marriage failing, losing your job, getting into an accident, children getting into trouble or some harm coming to them, losing your home, etc. Use your faith to overcome every element of fear!

"And because you belong to him, the power of the life-giving Spirit has freed you from the power of sin that leads to death."—Romans 8:2 (NLT)

The power God gives us to use is faith. Faith in God will overcome anything the world has to offer. However, it is up to us to get into the Word of God; to discover His will for us and to stand on that Word to receive what is promised to us. God's Word has the power to bring itself to pass. He promised us in Isaiah 55, "*So shall My word be that goes forth from My mouth; it shall not return to Me void, but it shall accomplish what I please, and it shall prosper in the thing for which I sent it.*" (vs. 11).

As Believers, we must believe and hold onto the truth of the Word. When we do, we have an ally in faith that is unstoppable...giving us no cause for fear. Of course, the enemy will use fear to get us to believe the promises of God will not happen for us, but we must resist the temptation to fear through faith and trust God every day of our lives!

"For the Spirit that God has given us does not make us timid; instead, his Spirit fills us with power, love, and self-control."—2 Timothy 1:7 (Good News Translation)

Fear gives power to death in our lives. I know that is a harsh statement but just stay with me one moment. Since the fall of Adam in the Garden of Eden, death has reigned on mankind. Death comes in many forms: whether it is the death of our physical bodies, the death of our health, the death of our marriages or family relationships, even the death of our financial well-being. Death brings breakdown and decay into our lives. Therefore, it must be understood, because of sin in this world we will face challenges; but God is not putting them on us and we must use our faith to see us through those times of difficulty in which we face.

When Adam sinned by disobeying God's command, two things happened. One, he broke fellowship with God and secondly, he turned the lordship of the earth over to Satan. God gave Adam the power and command to rule over the earth when He said: *"...Be fruitful, and multiply, and replenish the earth, and subdue it..."* but his disobedience to the command of God ended the authority and paradise they enjoyed, gave Satan their authority and introduced death into the earth.

God told Adam not to eat of the tree in the midst of the garden for, *"in the day that thou eatest thereof thou shalt surely die."*(Genesis 2:17). Of course they did not die immediately but their disobedience opened the door for the very spirit of death to enter them and the earth.

"The thief comes only in order to steal and kill and destroy. I came that they may have and enjoy life, and have it in abundance (to the full, till it overflows)."—John 10:10 (Amplified)

As mentioned before, death can come in many forms and it is represented by anything that God does not give us. Anything that steals, kills, or destroys is from the devil and God did not give it to us! To clarify this point, let's use guilt or condemnation for example. This is a form of death because its very existence can separate you from the presence of God. A condemned spirit will not allow you to walk in the freedom, love and forgiveness of

God. Under no circumstance is guilt or condemnation any good for anyone—saint and sinner alike. You have to remember this: God has forgiven you of all your fault and sin—you just have to receive it. Satan will do his best to remind you of your sin every day; and with each reminder you have to remind him that you are forgiven.

Where condemnation is concerned, fearing that you are not forgiven or will not be accepted is a lie and all lies come from the devil. You and I must trust God and His Word enough to receive His mercy that has been exhibited through the death of Jesus for the sin of the entire world. We all were doomed as sinners and condemned to die but the love of God reached out to us when we did not deserve it and gave us a chance to become His children. So, when we receive Christ's sacrifice for us, we receive everything that comes with it—including freedom from condemnation.

Let us use sickness and disease as our next example. As we are taught in scripture, *"...with his stripes we are healed"* (Isaiah 53:5; 1 Peter 2:24). Healed from what? We are healed from every sickness and disease known to man. God did not provide partial healing; nor did he only provide healing for a select few. In the body and through the blood of Jesus, healing was provided for all. So, why is there so much sickness?

First, sickness and disease is in the earth because of sin and will be here until God rids this earth of all sin…once and for all. Note I did not say your or my sin in particular, but sickness is here due to the original sin. Nevertheless, we can receive forgiveness of sin and the gift of righteousness by accepting Jesus as Lord of our lives. Doing this will cleanse us from all sin. Secondly, sickness and disease is so prevalent because we have been programmed to believe we "have to be sick", we "cannot avoid getting sick", "everybody get sick sometime", "this disease runs in my family" or "we have to die from something"…lies, Lies, ALL LIES!!

When we buy into the lie of the devil concerning sickness and disease, we will condition our hearts and minds to believe we do not have a choice over sickness. Consequently, we will be programmed to fear getting sick because we feel powerless to stand against it. But we are not powerless; God has given us power against all the power of the enemy. Yet, if we don't resist, we will have to deal with sickness in our bodies and its consequences the rest of our lives.

For our final example, let us look at poverty. People fear poverty because of everything that it brings…lack, shortage, borrowing, hunger, shame, poor health, crime, etc. In the Garden, there was no lack or shortage because God supplied everything His people needed. They needed not fear their needs will not be met because they knew God as a provider—for He had given them the best of everything in abundance.

Now, before you start to shift in that seat, bear with me for a moment. Like sickness, we have been conditioned to believe a couple of things that has to be dismissed right now. First, prosperity—not poverty—is God's will for each of His children. That's right, God wants us wealthy. How wealthy? Wealthy enough to make a difference in every life we come across.

You see, all through the Bible, God blessed His people abundantly. But, there is a prerequisite to this wealth; we must be willing, obedient and able to receive it. The Word declares in the Message Translation of Isaiah 1:19: *"If you'll willingly obey, you'll feast like kings."* Now, do not misunderstand this or me. God blesses us to show His love to His people and to enable us to be a greater witness to the world than we could ever be struggling.

Many people stay in the position of poverty and lack because either they do not know or believe it is the will of God for them to prosper. In either case, there is a solution. For those who don't know, they must hear the preaching of the true Gospel of the Kingdom. For the Kingdom of God is not impoverished and unable to pay its bills. But hearing preaching on the Gospel of the Kingdom alone is not enough. Those who hear must believe and receive the Word they hear.

Not knowing this truth or failure to believe it raises fear in the heart people and keep them chained to the reality of poverty and all of its effects. Now, you may say: "but I have a good job or business." It really does not make any difference how much money you make. If you are a slave to your job or business and cannot afford to make a real difference in the lives of people; or are afraid to take any time off to spend time with your family or before the Lord because you need the money; you, my friend, are deficient of all God intend for you.

Fear will keep you from trusting God where it counts the most—making a difference in the lives of others. God told Abraham He would "…bless thee and make thy name great; and thou shalt be a blessing" (Genesis 12:2). I want to ask you a question. Do you think this is being demonstrated in the world by Christians today; and if not, why not? It is because we have allowed the spirit of poverty to reign over us instead of us reigning over it. Having your bills paid and food on your table is not enough to be a living example of the love of God on this earth. In other words, having only your needs met is not a full example of God's faithfulness and proof of His blessing in our lives—there is so much more to it—for God wants this for everyone.

How can we truly tell people of the love of God without any demonstration? It is not enough to simply point at our life and say: 'look at how good God has been to me!' Now, that may work for one or even a few; but to really make an impact we should be able to demonstrate the love of God by meeting people at the point of their need and say with humility: 'I am able to pay your rent or car note because the Lord has truly blessed me'. When we do that, then we should be able to explain the goodness of God to them and how they can experience it in their lives also. This is evidence of the Kingdom of God at work in this world.

Consequently my friend, there is no reason to fear any of the ills and less than desirable things in life. We need to step away from fear and place our faith in God who truly wants us blessed in all aspects of our lives; and believe He absolutely cannot and will not fail.

Chapter 5

Faith and Our Words

22 "And Jesus answering saith unto them, Have faith in God. 23 For verily I say unto you, That whosoever shall say unto this mountain, Be thou removed, and be thou cast into the sea; and shall not doubt in his heart, but shall believe that those things which he saith shall come to pass; he shall have whatsoever he saith. 24 Therefore I say unto you, What things soever ye desire, when ye pray, believe that ye receive them, and ye shall have them."—Mark 11:21-24

The Effect of Our Words

The process of faith is to put what you believe into action by using your words as a creative force (vs. 23). It is not enough to express faith in God's Word only, but we must also have faith in the power of our words. God gave man creative power through the words of our mouths. If we truly understand this, would be careful of the words we speak. To put it simply, speak only what you want to come to pass. Because whether we realize it or not, we are getting those things that we are speaking.

Now the question is…what are we getting? The things we see and experience in our lives are pretty much an indication of the type of things we are speaking on a daily basis. If we do not like what we see in our lives (sickness, lack, etc.,), then we need to take inventory of the words that are coming out of our mouths. Because we are responsible for the words we speak.

"Death and life are in the power of the tongue: and they that love it shall eat the fruit thereof."—Proverbs 18:21

"What you say can preserve life or destroy it; so you must accept the consequences of your words."—Proverbs 18:21 (Good News Translation)

It is important to take note: there are "consequences" to speaking words which do not support our trust in the Word of God. Are you sick? Take a look at what you are saying. Do you spend a lot of time talking about what is always hurting or what diseases run in your family? If so, then that is exactly what you are creating in your life. Are you broke or cannot pay your bills? Then take a look at what you are saying. Do you spend a lot of time talking about what you cannot afford or how much everything costs and how little you have? Do you call yourself poor or broke? Do you joke about the lack in your life? Then do not be surprised if things are always tight and the bills keep coming. Change your words, change your life...your words are creative.

The words of your mouth are creating many of the circumstances of your life. Don't like what you have? Then change it by changing your words. Take a serious look at the words you are speaking. If you are speaking words of doubt, death, disaster, lack and impossibility, then change those to words of faith, life, protection, healing, abundance, and possibility. If you do, it will make a remarkable difference in your life.

Once we take command of the words we speak and make the decision to change the way we speak for the good, we will begin to see a transformation in our lives. It is God's Word coming out of our mouths in faith that moves mountains. God has given His Word the power to bring itself to pass. In Isaiah 55:11 the Lord tells us His Word: *"...always produces fruit..."*

After we practice reading, meditating and speaking in accordance with the Word, we will condition our hearts and minds to think and act like God's Word. We were created to be this way. Whenever you are facing death, speak life; sickness, speak healing and good health; darkness, speak light; or confusion, speak peace. This is putting your faith to action through words.

Speak What You Believe

"...all things are possible to him that believeth."
—Mark 9:23

Imagine facing something you would say was impossible to get through—we have all been there at one time or another. The father in the story that this verse is attached to was facing something totally frustrating. His son was completely taken over by a demon spirit. (Now, I do not know your opinion of the reality of demons—that is an issue for another time).

The point is, regardless of what you are facing, you can make it through it by having faith or believing in the unfailing Word of God. It is not enough to just say you believe or have faith—it is what you say and do while you believe. Both faith and believe are words that requires action. There is no way to do either without some effort on our part. That effort may be seen or not but it is required nonetheless.

The Bible tells us, *"...that faith without works is dead..."* (James 2:20). Does that mean that a person who does a lot of "works" is a person of faith? Not necessarily. But it does mean that someone who has Bible faith is a person who put action to their faith! One way we can put action to our faith is through using the God-given right and ability to use words. Jesus spoke to the fig tree and it responded. He told

His disciples, and us, that we could do the same thing if we would "Have faith in God". He also encourages us to believe on another level when He said: *"As far as possibilities go, everything is possible for the person who believes."*—Mark 9:23 (God's Word Translation). We have to believe the Word to see God's Will brought into the reality of our lives. What's more, it is our responsibility to believe God's Word to the point we believe it will come to pass without fail.

Nevertheless, we can only act and thereby receive to the level of our believing. Jesus told the blind men, *"According to your faith be it unto you."*—Matthew 9:29 (KJV). If we don't believe our words make a difference, we won't use them responsibly and purposefully to command change in our lives. Therefore, let us raise our level of believing and then raise our level of living by using our words to influence our lives and environment; thereby, becoming the co-creators of our world for good. Believe me, this pleases God!

"But what the scripture says about being put right with God through faith is this: "You are not to ask yourself, Who will go up into heaven?" (that is, to bring Christ down). 7 "Nor are you to ask, Who will go down into the world below?" (that is, to bring Christ up from death). 8 What it says is this: "God's message is near you, on your lips and in your heart"—that is, the

message of faith that we preach."—Romans 10:6-8 (Good News Translation)

God gives us the right to use our words to exercise the creative nature of God within us! The Bible teaches us that we are made in the image of God and after His likeness. This likeness or similarity is not in physical characteristics as much as spiritual, because God is Spirit and not natural or human. The spiritual nature of God removes Him out of this three-dimensional world we live in and places Him on another plane or sphere. Not necessarily far from us but definitely different. In this way, He sees and speaks from the world of the spirit and is not moved by the conditions of this physical world.

One of the attributes of God is reflected in the fact: He used words to create this world. We find in the Genesis account that God called everything into existence before its physical form was established. This calling forth of something, gave presence spiritually, before it could be seen in the natural, and then it appeared. In other words, God knew what He wanted to be and then said, "Let there be..." for everything He created. But when He got to man, He became descriptive and described our nature and realm of authority by saying: *"Let us make man in our image, after our likeness: and let them have dominion..."*—Genesis 1:26

Therefore, God created man as spirit first before clothing him in flesh, and gave him the ability to speak and create like Himself. That is why it is necessary for us to take control of our thought-life and belief system. Because if we do not submit our hearts and minds to God and the way He intend for things to be, we will by default be submitting to Satan's intentions—which are never for our good.

This is why Satan will try to influence our thoughts and words to get us to agree with him and his purpose. He is not a creator and cannot create anything. So, he has to get us to enter into partnership with him by using our creative ability and speaking the words of death—rather than life.

Satan is a destroyer and, contrary to some opinions, he has to have our permission to wreak havoc in our lives. We give him this permission by agreeing with him, first in our minds and then with our words. He cannot do anything to us, but he can and does suggest very strongly, and far too often we listen. When we do listen and then begin to say what he is saying, we give him authority in our lives and atmosphere. But we have a choice…

"So then, submit yourselves to God. Resist the Devil, and he will run away from you."—James 4:7 (GNT)

The minute we resist Satan and his advances he will leave or "flee" from us; at that point, we can

use our God-given ability and right to speak what
we want to come to pass. We can do this by
believing in God and His Word. One of the main
examples is given to us is in the "model prayer",
otherwise known as The Lord's Prayer. In this,
Jesus directs us to pray "Thy Kingdom come. Thy
will be done in earth, as it is in heaven" (Matt.
6:10). It is our responsibility to advance the
Kingdom of God here on earth. We do that through
prayer and confession when we understand the will
of God. We can only do this effectively when we
spend adequate time in God's Word. Doing this,
will allow the Word to be planted on the inside of
us and become a part of our very being. Therefore,
let us remember these things:

(1) God loves us;

(2) God has a plan for us;

(3) God wants us to walk in faith and not fear;
and

(4) God has given us the creative power of
words to co-create the world we live in.

Finally, the Word of God has the power to bring
itself to pass and it will be a creative force in our
lives when we place our faith in it and speak it. At
no time has God spoken anything that it did not
happen, take place or come into being. So
everything that we find in the Word was spoken by

God and it exists in the spiritual realm waiting for us to speak it into existence into this earth's realm.

God has done his part; it is time for us to do ours—HAVE FAITH IN GOD!

Prayer for Salvation and Baptism in the Holy Spirit

"All that the Father giveth me shall come to me; and him that cometh to me I will in no wise cast out."—John 6:37

Heavenly Father, I come to You in the Name of Jesus. Your Word says, "Whosoever shall call on the name of the Lord shall be saved" (Acts 2:21). I am calling on You. I pray and ask Jesus to come into my heart and be Lord over my life according to Romans 10:9-10:

9 "That if thou shalt confess with thy mouth the Lord Jesus, and shalt believe in thine heart that God hath raised him from the dead, thou shalt be saved. 10 For with the heart man believeth unto righteousness; and with the mouth confession is made unto salvation."

I now confess that Jesus is Lord, and I believe in my heart that God raised Him from the dead. I now receive Jesus as Lord over my life and confess that I am now reborn—I am a Christian—a child of Almighty God! I am saved!

You also said in Your Word, "If ye then, being evil, know how give good gifts unto your children: how much more shall your heavenly Father give the Holy Spirit to them that ask Him?" (Luke 11:13). Therefore Lord, I'm also asking You to fill me with the Holy Spirit. I now receive the Holy Spirit by faith; and say, Holy Spirit, rise up within me as I praise God. I fully expect to speak with other tongues as You give me the utterance (Act 2:4), in Jesus' Name…Amen!

Now, begin to praise God for filling you with the Holy Spirit. Speak those words and syllables you receive—not in your own language, but the language given to you by the Holy Spirit. You have to use your own voice. God will not force you to speak. Don't be concerned with how it sounds. It is a heavenly language! Continue with the blessing god has given you and pray in the Spirit every day.

Now, you are a born-again, Spirit-filled Believer. You'll never be the same! Find a good church fellowship that boldly preaches God's Word and obeys it. Get yourself a good study bible that you can understand and begin to read and study the Word every day.

About the Author

Sebastian, an ordained gospel minister for over thirty years, is the founder and minister of Faith1st and Sebastian Weaver Ministries. He and his wife reside in Atlanta, Georgia and are the proud parents of six young adults—whom they love dearly.

He has devoted his life to being a minister of reconciliation and helping people in their discovery of: God's will for their lives, their walk of faith, and finding solutions to the struggles of life—especially in the area of marriage and healing.

www.ingramcontent.com/pod-product-compliance
Lightning Source LLC
Chambersburg PA
CBHW060616030426
42337CB00018B/3069